QUOTES
for
CONSERVATIVES

QUOTES
for
CONSERVATIVES

WIT, WISDOM, AND INSIGHT
FROM CONSERVATIVES
THROUGHOUT HISTORY

✦✦✦★✦✦✦

Edited and Illustrated by

GARRY APGAR

CENTER STREET

New York   Nashville

Center Street
Hachette Book Group
1290 Avenue of the Americas, New York, NY 10104
centerstreet.com
twitter.com/centerstreet

First Edition: March 2020

Center Street is a division of Hachette Book Group, Inc. The Center Street name and logo are trademarks of Hachette Book Group, Inc.

The publisher is not responsible for websites (or their content) that are not owned by the publisher.

The Hachette Speakers Bureau provides a wide range of authors for speaking events. To find out more, go to www.HachetteSpeakersBureau.com or call (866) 376-6591.

Library of Congress Cataloging-in-Publication Data has been applied for.

ISBNs: 978-1-5460-8588-1 (paper over board), 978-1-5460-8589-8(ebook)

Printed in the United States of America

LSC-C

10   9   8   7   6   5   4   3   2   1

Glenn Beck: What makes America great?
Foxworthy: The spirit of its people.

Jeff Foxworthy (1958–), comedian. (On the Glenn Beck
show [CNN], March 21, 2008)

PREFACE

Quotes for Conservatives is not so much a collection of quotations as it is a collection of ideas. Just as words are building blocks of sentences, memorable sentences, skillfully constructed—the very definition of a good quote—serve as powerful tools in the formulation and communication of ideas. And of course, ideas, sharply opposed to one another, lie at the heart of our seemingly endless political and cultural wrangling in the Age of Trump.

Quotes for Conservatives contains nearly 300 entries grouped under 92 headings focused on topics and individuals of enduring or intense current interest in the realms of history, morals and commerce as well as politics and culture. Subject headings like "Atheism," "Business," "Fake News," "Hollywood," "Patriotism" and "Virtue Signaling," and sections devoted to major public figures like Lincoln, Ronald Reagan, Margaret Thatcher, the Clintons and Donald Trump.

Quotes for Conservatives is unique in other ways.

Standard dictionaries of quotations cover the waterfront, going back to the Bible and ancient Greece and Rome. Virtually every item in *Quotes for Conservatives* is thoroughly modern. Many never before collected in print or online, others never accurately cited or sourced. The vast majority of the "quotees" are American, and roughly sixty per cent of the quotes—153 out of 272—have been gleaned from words spoken, written or diffused electronically over the last twenty years.

They all have something wise or insightful, often witty, to say about what Charles Krauthammer called Things That Matter. For example, the Second Amendment, which according to Rush Limbaugh exists "in case the government fails to follow the first one." Or Charlton Heston's remark that "Political correctness is tyranny with manners."

Although conservatives comprise the core "target" audience of *Quotes for Conservatives*, anyone—liberals and progressives included—who cares about Things That Matter should find joy within these pages. (And a chuckle or two from the twenty-two cartoons that accompany the quotes.)

Rush Limbaugh, Charles Krauthammer and Ronald Reagan, together, have the lion's share of entries in *Quotes for Conservatives*. But not every voice comes from the right. Among the exceptions are Supreme Court Justice William Brennan, President John F. Kennedy, and 2016 Hillary supporter Richard Branson, founder of Virgin Atlantic. "One thing is certain in business," Branson says, "You and everyone around you will make mistakes." Even further afield is Edward Snowden, the ex-CIA employee and alleged Russian spy, who in 2014 declared: "There's definitely a deep state. Trust me, I've been there."

As political and cultural discord rages unabated across the fruited plain, long-held beliefs and assumptions are being put to the test, left and right. Careful consideration of the ideas conveyed in *Quotes for Conservatives* can help clarify and ameliorate some of the contentious issues that divide us as a nation. Whether you like or loathe the persons quoted in this book, this much is certain: a good quotation makes you think...and sometimes makes you re-think what you think you already know. That is not a bad thing.

Garry Apgar

AMERICA

America is a vast conspiracy to make you happy.

> *John Updike (1932–2009), novelist, critic ("How to Love*
> *America and Leave It at the Same Time,"* New Yorker,
> *August 19, 1972)*

— —

America is not a place. It is a dream.

> *Clotaire Rapaille (1941–), French marketing consultant*
> *(quoted in Jack Hitt, "Does the Smell of Coffee Brewing*
> *Remind You of Your Mother?,"* New York Times,
> *May 7, 2000)*

— —

America is the only country ever founded on an idea. The only country that is not founded on race or even common history. It's founded on an idea and the idea is liberty.

> *Charles Krauthammer (1950-2018), opinion writer.*
> *"The Wisdom of Charles Krauthammer," posted one day*
> *after his death, June 22, 2018, on* FoxNews.com.

AMERICA FIRST

I am not speaking in a selfish spirit when I say that our whole duty, for the present, at any rate, is summed up in the motto: "America first." Let us think of America before we think of Europe, in order that America may be fit to be Europe's friend when the day of tested friendship comes.

Woodrow Wilson (1856–1924), Princeton University president, president of the United States (remarks at Associated Press headquarters, New York, April 20, 1915, after World War I had begun, but before America joined the fight in 1917)

When we say we will put America first, we mean also that our Judeo-Christian values are going to be preserved, and our Western heritage is going to be handed down to future generations, not dumped onto some landfill called multiculturalism.

Patrick J. Buchanan (1938–), advisor to Presidents Nixon, Ford, and Reagan, opinion writer (speech in Concord, New Hampshire, December 10, 1991, during Buchanan's unsuccessful campaign for the Republican presidential nomination in 1992)

AMERICAN EXCEPTIONALISM

President Obama was asked about American exceptionalism. His answer? "I believe in American exceptionalism, just as I suspect that the Brits believe in British exceptionalism and the Greeks believe in Greek exceptionalism." Interesting response. Because if everyone is exceptional, no one is.

Charles Krauthammer (1950–2018), opinion writer ("Decline Is a Choice," lecture at the Manhattan Institute for Policy Research, New York, October 5, 2009)

America is not exceptional because it has long attempted to be a force for good in the world, it attempts to be a force for good because it is exceptional.

Peggy Noonan (1950–), speechwriter for President Reagan, opinion writer ("Vladimir Putin Takes Exception," Wall Street Journal, September 13, 2013)

AMERICAN REVOLUTION

It is the object only of war that makes it honourable. And if there was ever *a just* war since the world began, it is this which America is now engaged in.

Thomas Paine (1737–1809), English-born patriot, polemicist
*(*The American Crisis, *no. 5, March 21, 1778)*

———

The American Revolution was utterly lacking in the messianic, bloody-minded idealism of the French. It rearranged the constitutional furniture. Its revolutionary leaders died in their own beds. What kind of revolution was that?

Charles Krauthammer (1950–2018), opinion writer
("A Failed Revolution," Washington Post, *July 14, 1989)*

———

The American Revolution was a political, not a social, revolution; it was about emancipating individuals for the pursuit of happiness, not about the state allocating wealth and opportunity. Hence our exceptional Constitution, which says not what government must do for Americans but what it cannot do to them.

George F. Will (1941–), opinion writer ("A Congress That Reasserts Its Power," Washington Post, *January 16, 2011)*

ATHEISM

I have heard an atheist defined as a man who has no invisible means of support.

John Buchan (1875–1940), Scottish-born novelist (speech at the annual dinner of London's Company of City Solicitors, February 21, 1935)

No man knows enough about the conditions of existence to know for certain that there is no God.

Michael Novak (1933–2017), Catholic philosopher, ambassador to the United Nations Commission on Human Rights ("The Truth About Religious Freedom," First Things, March 2006)

Atheists are free to choose. What they're not free to do is attack the very culture/religion that guarantees them that freedom.

Michael Walsh (1949–), critic, author, screenwriter (interview with Kathryn Jean Lopez, "Hush Now and Listen for the Better Angels," National Review Online, December 20, 2018)

BIRTHRIGHT CITIZENSHIP

Birthright citizenship provides a powerful magnet for people to violate our immigration laws and undermines the plenary power over naturalization that the Constitution explicitly gives to Congress.

John Eastman (1960–), constitutional law professor, Chapman University, and senior fellow, Claremont Institute ("Birthright Citizenship Is Not Actually in the Constitution," New York Times, *December 22, 2015)*

Children born in the United States should be deemed Americans only if their parents are U.S. persons—that is, either U.S. citizens or lawful-permanent-resident aliens.

Andrew McCarthy (1962–), former assistant United States attorney, contributing editor, National Review *("The 14th Amendment Does Not Mandate Birthright Citizenship,"* National Review Online, *November 3, 2018)*

BORDERS

The simple truth is that we've lost control of our own borders, and no nation can do that and survive.

> *Ronald Reagan (1911–2004), actor, governor of California, president of the United States (White House press conference, June 14, 1984)*

A nation WITHOUT BORDERS is not a nation at all. We must have a wall. The rule of law matters.

> *Donald Trump (1946–), real estate developer, television personality, president of the United States (on Twitter, @realDonaldTrump, July 28, 2015)*

There is no "immigration crisis"—other, that is, than the crisis of our too-porous borders.

> *Roger Kimball (1953–), editor, author, publisher, The New Criterion ("The Trump Resistance™ Has Lost Its Mind!," USA.Spectator.co.uk, June 20, 2018)*

BUREAUCRACY

There is…no surer method of economising and saving money than in the reduction of the number of officials.

> *Winston Churchill (1874–1965), British statesman (in the House of Commons, April 24, 1928)*

The only good bureaucrat is one with a pistol at his head. Put it in his hand and it's good-bye to the Bill of Rights.

> *H. L. Mencken (1880–1956), journalist, editor ("A Time to Be Wary," Baltimore Evening Sun, March 13, 1933)*

A government bureau is the nearest thing to eternal life we'll ever see on this earth.

> *Ronald Reagan (1911–2004), actor, governor of California, president of the United States ("A Time for Choosing," nationally televised address in support of Barry Goldwater's presidential campaign, October 27, 1964)*

BUSINESS

Business was originated to produce happiness, not to pile up millions.

B. C. Forbes (1880–1954), Scottish-born journalist, founder of Forbes *magazine ("The Pursuit of Happiness," editorial in* Forbes, *September 15, 1917)*

— —

The chief business of the American people is business.

Calvin Coolidge (1872–1933), Massachusetts governor, vice president, and president of the United States (Speech to the American Society of Newspaper Editors, Washington, D.C., January 17, 1925)

— —

One thing is certain in business: You and every one around you will make mistakes.

Richard Branson (1950—), English entrepreneur, philanthropist (Business Stripped Bare: Adventures of a Global Entrepreneur [2008], in the chapter "Learning from Mistakes and Setbacks: Damage Report")

CAPITALISM

Free competition is worth more to society than it costs.

> *Oliver Wendell Holmes Jr. (1841–1935), associate Supreme Court justice (Supreme Court of Massachusetts, Vegelahn v. Guntner, decided October 26, 1896)*

— • —

I do not report on the benefits of free markets because I like "making real money"…I report on them because freedom has lifted more people out of poverty than government dictates ever will.

> *John Stossel (1947–), libertarian host of ABC's 20/20 and the Fox Business Channel program Stossel (letter to the editor, The Nation, January 23, 2002)*

— • —

Creativity is the foundation of capitalism.

> *George Gilder (1939–), economist (on the Fox News Channel program Life, Liberty & Levin, October 14, 2018)*

CELEBRITY

★★★

Celebrity-worship and hero-worship should not be confused. Yet we confuse them every day, and by doing so we come dangerously close to depriving ourselves of all real models. We lose sight of the men and women who do not simply seem great because they are famous but are famous because they are great.

> *Daniel Boorstin (1914–2004), Librarian of Congress (The Image: Or, What Happened to the American Dream [1961], ch. 2)*

— • —

Celebrity is a corrosive condition for the soul.

> *Charlton Heston (1923–2008), actor, National Rifle Association president (interview with Jani Allan, "Charlton Heston: Great Sport with a Line in Heroic Role Models," The Sunday Times, June 17, 1990)*

— • —

The resource upon which the media and entertainment industry depends is not fame but its toxic run-off, celebrity.

> *P. J. O'Rourke (1947—), humorist, essayist, novelist (Here's a Tax We Can All Agree On," Weekly Standard, May 30, 2005)*

CHURCH AND STATE

Leave the matter of religion to the family altar, the church and the private school, supported entirely by private contributions. Keep the church and state forever separate.

Ulysses S. Grant (1822–1885), Union Army commanding general in the Civil War, president of the United States (speech to the Army of the Tennessee, Des Moines, Iowa, September 30, 1875)

———

Today courts wrongly interpret separation of church and state to mean that religion has no place in the public arena, or that morality derived from religion should not be permitted to shape our law. Somehow freedom for religious expression has become freedom from religious expression.

Dinesh D'Souza (1961–), author, documentary filmmaker (What's So Great About Christianity [2008], ch. 5)

WINSTON CHURCHILL

We are all worms, but I do believe I am a glow worm.

> *Winston Churchill (1874–1965), British statesman (to Lady Violet Asquith, circa 1906–1907, quoted in William Manchester and Paul Reid,* The Last Lion: Winston Spencer Churchill: Defender of the Realm, 1940–1965 *[2012], part seven)*

His belief in and predilection for the American democracy are too well known to need comment—they are the foundation of his political outlook.

> *Isaiah Berlin (1909–1997), British philosopher ("Mr. Churchill,"* Atlantic Monthly, *September 1949)*

In the dark days and darker nights when Britain stood alone—and most men save Englishmen despaired of England's life—he mobilized the English language and sent it into battle.

> *John F. Kennedy (1917–1963), Massachusetts senator, president of the United States (at a White House ceremony conferring honorary American citizenship on Churchill, April 9, 1963)*

THE CLINTONS

I remember him as very gregarious, never in class, always talking to someone out in the hallway or in the dining room or something like that. I remember her as a very rigid, unfriendly, hard-core left-winger.

> *John Bolton (1948—), National Security advisor to President Trump and student classmate at Yale of both Clintons in the early 1970s ("The Man with the Mustache," interview with Jay Nordlinger in* National Review, *December 31, 2010)*

The Clintons are creeps and liars and scoundrels and misfits, always have been, always will be. They are the penicillin-resistant syphilis of American politics.

> *Kevin D. Williamson (1972–), libertarian opinion writer ("Next!,"* National Review Online, *March 8, 2015)*

The Clintons lie when they do not have to lie, and they tell a gaudy whopper when a little white lie would be perfectly satisfactory.

> *R. Emmett Tyrrell Jr. (1943–), editor in chief,* The American Spectator *(quoting himself in "Cataloguing the Clinton Lies,"* Washington Times, *December 29, 2015)*

COLD WAR

★★★

Some people think I'm simplistic, but there's a difference between being simplistic and being simple. My theory of the Cold War is that we win and they lose. What do you think about that?

> *Ronald Reagan (1911–2004), actor, governor of California, president of the United States (conversation, early January 1977, with Richard Allen, later Reagan's national security advisor, quoted in Henry R. Nau, "Ronald Reagan," in* US Foreign Policy and Democracy Promotion: From Theodore Roosevelt to Barack Obama *[2013], edited by Michael Cox)*

▬◄

Neoconservatism is a product of the Cold War. It's understandable that neoconservative intellectuals who helped win the Cold War might want to hold onto the label, but it's time to give it a comfortable retirement in the history books.

> *Jonah Goldberg (1969–), opinion writer,* National Review Online *editor-at-large ("The Term 'Neocon' Has Run Its Course,"* National Review Online, *January 6, 2016)*

CONGRESS

"The chances are that a man cannot get into Congress now without resorting to arts and means that should render him unfit to go there."

Mark Twain (1835–1910), writer, humorist (Philip Sterling, a character in Twain's novel co-authored with Charles Dudley Warner, The Gilded Age *[1873], ch. 50)*

Let me tell you something: They say he lied to Congress. I can think of no better bunch of people to lie to than Congress.

Rush Limbaugh (1951—), talk show host (on The Rush Limbaugh Show, *June 6, 1994, talking about Lt. Colonel Oliver North)*

If lawmakers do not like the laws that we enforce, that we are charged to enforce, that we are sworn to enforce, then they should have the courage and the skill to change those laws. Otherwise, they should shut up and support the men and women on the front lines.

John F. Kelly (1950–), retired Marine Corps general, chief of staff to President Trump (speech as secretary of the Department of Homeland Security, George Washington University, April 18, 2017)

CONSERVATISM

What is conservatism? Is it not adherence to the old and tried, against the new and untried?

> *Abraham Lincoln (1809–1865), first Republican president of the United States (Cooper Union speech, New York City, February 27, 1860)*

The facts of life are Conservative.

> *Quentin Hogg, a.k.a. Lord Hailsham (1907–2001), chairman of the British Conservative Party, Lord Chancellor (quoted in "The New Socialism," Punch, January 10, 1968)*

A conservative is a liberal who was mugged the night before.

> *Frank Rizzo (1920–1991), Democrat mayor of Philadelphia (quoted in "The Causes of Crime," Time, June 30, 1975)*

I personally think conservatism is the glue that holds society together.

> *Mark Levin (1957–), talk show host (on his Fox News Channel program, Life, Liberty & Levin, August 26, 2018)*

THE CONSTITUTION

It has been the most successful conservative device in the history of the world.

Russell Kirk (1918–1994), political and social theorist (The Conservative Mind: From Burke to Santayana [1953], ch. 3)

— —

I think that the Constitution itself, the written document, is the ultimate stare decisis.

Clarence Thomas (1948–), associate Supreme Court justice (commenting on "stare decisis," the legal principle of upholding precedent, at a Heritage Foundation event in Washington, D.C., October 26, 2016)

— —

The framers established that the Constitution is designed to secure the blessings of liberty.

Brett Kavanaugh (1965–), Supreme Court justice (at the White House, July 9, 2018, accepting his nomination by President Trump to serve on the court)

Culture

It is the constitutional privilege of every American to become cultured or to just grow up like Donald Duck.

Walt Disney (1901–1966), producer of animated and live-action films, creator of the destination theme park (speaking at intermission during a Texaco–Metropolitan Opera radio broadcast of the Barber of Seville, *March 1, 1941)*

Culture may even be described simply as that which makes life worth living.

*T. S. Eliot (1888–1965), poet, essayist, critic (*Notes Towards a Definition of Culture *[1948], ch. 3)*

Politics is downstream from culture.

Andrew Breitbart (1969–2012), libertarian founder, Breitbart.com *(quoted in Steve Oney, "Citizen Breitbart: The Web's New Right-Wing Impresario,"* Time, *March 25, 2010)*

DATA

★★★

If you torture the data enough, nature will always confess.

Ronald H. Coase (1910–2013), English-born economics professor, University of Chicago (Essays on Economics and Economists *[1994], ch. 2*)

――

The plural of anecdote is data.

Ben Wattenberg (1933–2015), PBS host, political commentator, American Enterprise Institute senior fellow (Values Matter Most: How Republicans, or Democrats, or a Third Party Can Win and Renew the American Way of Life *[1995], ch. 16*)

――

"Using statistics," my teacher used to say, "is like driving a car down a road with the windshield blacked out, guided only by your rear-view mirror."

Richard Fernandez (circa 1945—), Filipino-born Australian software designer and blogger ("Rear Window," Belmont Club [PJMedia.com], November 13, 2013)

DECLARATION OF INDEPENDENCE

America is the only nation in the world that is founded on a creed. That creed is set forth with dogmatic and even theological lucidity in the Declaration of Independence; perhaps the only piece of practical politics that is also theoretical politics and also great literature.

> *G. K. Chesterton (1874–1936), English journalist, critic, philosopher (*What I Saw in America *[1922], in the chapter "What Is America?")*

— —

We believe that American conservatism has something special to conserve. That something is formed around the Declaration of Independence.

> *Larry P. Arnn (1952–), president of Hillsdale College (preface to Harry V. Jaffa,* Storm Over the Constitution *[1999])*

— —

The Declaration of Independence set liberty, ordained by our Creator and inseparable from our equality, in black and white, at the top of our national birth certificate.

> *Richard Brookhiser (1955—), conservative writer and biographer (*Give Me Liberty: A History of America's Exceptional Idea *[2019], "Conclusion")*

DECLINE AND FALL

★★★

Perhaps it is historically true that no order of society ever perishes save by its own hand.

> *John Maynard Keynes (1883–1946), English economist (*The Economic Consequences of the Peace *[1919], ch. 6)*

— —

Cultures do decline, and sometimes die.

> *Robert Bork (1927–2012), Yale Law School professor, federal judge (*Slouching Towards Gomorrah: Modern Liberalism and American Decline *[1996], "Introduction")*

— —

Decline is a choice. Principles, like gods, die when no one believes in them anymore.

> *Jonah Goldberg (1969–), opinion writer,* National Review Online *editor-at-large (*Suicide of the West: How the Rebirth of Tribalism, Populism, Nationalism, and Identity Politics Is Destroying American Democracy *[2018], "Conclusion")*

DEEP STATE

There's definitely a deep state. Trust me, I've been there.

> *Edward Snowden (1983–), ex-CIA computer specialist,*
> *accused spy (quoted in Katrina vanden Heuvel and Stephen*
> *F. Cohen, "Edward Snowden: A 'Nation' Interview," The*
> *Nation, October 28, 2014)*

The Deep State—The successful outcome of cultural Marxism is a bureaucratic state beholden to no one, certainly not the American people.

> *Rich Higgins (circa 1974–), former National Security*
> *Council director for strategic planning under President*
> *Trump ("POTUS & Political Warfare," seven-page memo,*
> *May 2017, circulated among a select number of friends and*
> *Trump administration staff)*

The #DeepState is deeper than we feared. It will stop at nothing to undermine the #conservative agenda.

> *Jay Sekulow (1956–), chief counsel, American Center for*
> *Law & Justice, and legal advisor to President Trump (on*
> *Twitter, @JaySekulow, August 24, 2018)*

Democratic Party

★★★

When you're a hammer, everything is a nail. When you're a Democrat, everything is Watergate.

Michael Goodwin (circa 1950–), New York Times *reporter,* New York Post *columnist ("Why James Comey Had to Go,"* New York Post, *May 9, 2017)*

━ ━

The Political Party That Is Never Wrong.

R. Emmett Tyrrell Jr. (1943–), editor in chief, The American Spectator *("The Democratic Party, the Party of Resistance,"* Washington Times, *September 11, 2018)*

━ ━

The Democrats don't seem to understand what it is they are really fighting, which, in no small part, is not the Republicans but the constitutional architecture of the United States.

Kevin D. Williamson (1972–), libertarian opinion writer ("What the Midterm Results Mean," National Review Online, *November 7, 2018)*

DIVERSITY

The next time some academics tell you how important "diversity" is, ask how many Republicans there are in their sociology department.

> *Thomas Sowell (1930–), economist, Hoover Institution*
> *senior fellow ("Random Thoughts," Jewish World Review,*
> *July 31, 1998)*

Diversity to them is looking different and thinking alike.

> *Harry Stein (1948–), writer and humorist, talking about*
> *the "multiple hypocrisies" of the Left (quoted in Bernard*
> *Chapin, "The Intolerance of the Left," Conservative*
> *Crusader, June 26, 2009)*

Progressives celebrate diversity in everything but thought.

> *George F. Will (1941–), opinion writer ("Those Pesky Things*
> *Called Laws," Washington Post, March 9, 2012)*

ELITISM

Between New York and L.A. there are 200 million people who aren't hip, and they don't want to be.

> *Jeff Foxworthy (1958–), comedian (quoted in Jon Matsumoto, "You Might Be a TV Star If…," Los Angeles Times, December 23, 1995)*

— —

You might say the road to Hell is paved with Ivy League degrees.

> *Thomas Sowell (1930–), economist, Hoover Institution senior fellow (on Uncommon Knowledge with Peter Robinson, produced by the Hoover Institution and posted online, January 25, 2012)*

— —

Civilizations rot from the head down. It's the elitists that go first. It's the elitists that have a death wish. It's the elitists that have this sense that we have to prove something, that the common people are just a bunch of low, you know, those—what do they call it?—those low sloping foreheads.

> *Bill Whittle (1959–), conservative political commentator ("Civilization in Crisis," talk at the Conservative Forum of Silicon Valley, Mountain View, California, May 7, 2013)*

ENTERTAINMENT ELITES

In the United States of Entertainment there is no greater sin than to bore the audience.

> *Bernard Goldberg (1945–), former CBS News reporter,*
> *conservative author (*Bias: A CBS Insider Exposes How the
> Media Distort the News *[2001], ch. 1)*

— —

Entertainment elites are sealed off *physically* by means of limos and velvet ropes, cultural elites like Susan Sontag and Norman Mailer insulate themselves intellectually from the masses.

> *Laura Ingraham (1963–), host of* The Ingraham Angle
> on the Fox News Channel *(*Shut Up and Sing: How Elites
> from Hollywood, Politics, and the Media are Subverting
> America *[2003], ch. 1)*

— —

I've been to shows where people start haranguing the audience about what's going on politically and I'm thinking, "You know, this isn't why I came here."

> *Billy Joel (1949–), musician (quoted in Patrick Doyle,*
> *"Doubt, Trump and Finally Becoming Cool,"* Rolling Stone,
> *June 14, 2017)*

EQUALITY

★★★

Equal, *adj.* As bad as something else.

Ambrose Bierce (1842–1914), journalist, humorist
("Editorial," The San Francisco Illustrated Wasp,
May 2, 1884)

— —

A society that puts equality—in the sense of outcome—ahead of freedom will end up with neither equality nor freedom.

Milton Friedman (1912–2006), economics professor,
University of Chicago, Hoover Institution senior fellow
(Free to Choose: A Personal Statement *[1980], ch. 5,*
co-authored with Rose Friedman)

— —

We have a much higher attachment to the idea of liberty than we do equality. There is no Statue of Equality in New York Harbor. It's the Statue of Liberty. We're different that way.

Charles Krauthammer (1950–2018), opinion writer (on the
Fox News Channel program Tucker Carlson Tonight,
July 24, 2017)

European Union

$\star\star\star$

When I go into Downing Street they do what I say; when I go to Brussels they take no notice.

> *Rupert Murdoch (1931–), Australian-born media mogul (to Anthony Hilton, city editor,* Times of London, *in the early 1980s. Murdoch later said he "never uttered those words." Robert Booth and Jane Martinson, "Rupert Murdoch: 'I've Never Asked any Prime Minister for Anything,'"* The Guardian, *December 19, 2016.)*

— —

That such an unnecessary and irrational project as building a European superstate was ever embarked upon will seem in future years to be perhaps the greatest folly of the modern era.

> *Margaret Thatcher (1925–2013), British prime minister (*Statecraft: Strategies for a Changing World *[2002], ch. 10)*

— —

The European Union is dying before your very eyes.

> *Nigel Farage (1964–), member of the European Parliament, founder of the Brexit political party (interview on the Fox Business Network program* Varney & Company, *December 2, 2016.*

EVOLUTION

★★★

No matter what argument you make against evolution, the response is, *Well, you know, it's possible to believe in evolution and believe in God.* Yes, and it's possible to believe in Spiderman and believe in God, but that doesn't prove Spiderman is true.

Ann Coulter (1961–), writer, commentator (Godless: The Church of Liberalism [2002], ch. 10)

—   —

Evolution and creationism both require faith. It's just a matter of where you choose to place that faith.

Ben Carson (1951–), neurosurgeon, Johns Hopkins Hospital, and secretary of Housing and Urban Development in the Trump administration (keynote address at the annual National Science Teachers Association convention, Philadelphia, March 27, 2003)

—   —

To say that animals evolved into man is like saying that Carrara marble evolved into Michelangelo's *David*.

Tom Wolfe (1931–2018), writer (The Kingdom of Speech [2016], ch. 6)

Fake News

Where news is concerned, always await the sacrament of confirmation.

> *Voltaire (1694–1778), French* philosophe *and writer (Letter to the comte d'Argental, August 28, 1760)*

The FAKE NEWS media (failing @nytimes, @NBCNews, @ABC, @CBS, @CNN) is not my enemy, it is the enemy of the American People!

> *Donald Trump (1946–), real estate developer, television personality, president of the United States (on Twitter, @realDonaldTrump, February 17, 2017)*

President Trump has misdiagnosed what's wrong with the media. It's not deliberate "fakery," but a tsunami of too much news badly edited, if edited at all. We're awash in information, much of it show-biz trivia that we don't need.

> *Wesley Pruden (1935–2019), editor in chief,* Washington Times *("Mainstream Media Are Awash in a Tsunami of Trivia,"* Washington Times, *July 19, 2018)*

FASCISM

The people who have shown the best understanding of Fascism are either those who have suffered under it or those who have a Fascist streak in themselves.

> *George Orwell (1903–1950), English journalist, author*
> *("Wells, Hitler and the World State,"* Horizon, *August 1941)*

—ー —ー

One of the great unexplained phenomena of modern astronomy: namely, that the dark night of fascism is always descending in the United States and yet only lands in Europe.

> *Tom Wolfe (1931–2018), writer ("The Intelligent Coed's*
> *Guide to America,"* Harper's, *July 1976)*

—ー —ー

We've come to use the word "fascist" as a substitute for "evil" or "bad."

> *Jonah Goldberg (1969–), author and opinion writer*
> *("What 'The Daily Show' Cut Out: Liberals Who Brand*
> *Conservatives as Fascists Need to Take a Look at History,"*
> Los Angeles Times, *January 22, 2008)*

FREEDOM OF SPEECH

Freedom of speech means freedom for those who you despise, and freedom to express the most despicable views. It also means that the government cannot pick and choose which expressions to authorize and which to prevent.

> *Alan Dershowitz (1938–), Harvard Law School professor emeritus ("Are Radical Imams Going to Redefine Freedom of Speech?,"* Huffington Post, *November 20, 2012)*

The First Amendment does not give you the right to commit a crime.

> *Jeanine Pirro (1951–), former district attorney, author, and host of the Fox News show* Justice with Judge Jeanine *(*Justice with Judge Jeanine, *February 4, 2017, "My Opening Statement")*

Freedom of speech is an important pillar of our nation's founding principles and a free press is important to our democracy. The press should be fair, unbiased and responsible.

> *Melania Trump (1970–), fashion model, First Lady of the United States (comment for CNN reporter Kate Bennett, posted on Twitter, @KateBennett_DC, May 30, 2018)*

BARRY GOLDWATER

★★★

We—27,178,188 of us—who voted for him in 1964 believe he won, it just took 16 years to count the votes.

George F. Will (1941–), opinion writer (talking about Ronald Reagan's election as president in 1980, "The Cheerful Malcontent," Washington Post, *May 31, 1998)*

— —

Unlike nearly every other politician who ever lived, anywhere in the world, Barry Goldwater always said exactly what was on his mind. He spared his listeners nothing.

Lloyd Grove (1955–), editor-at-large, The Daily Beast *("Goldwater Nuggets,"* Washington Post, *May 30, 1998)*

— —

I guess you could call him the John the Baptist of our movement.

Ronald Reagan (1911–2004), actor, governor of California, president of the United States (quoted in Patrick J. Buchanan, "Is Trump the Heir to Reagan?," TownHall.com, *October 14, 2007)*

GOVERNMENT

It is an age-old Washington axiom that there is nothing so permanent as a temporary government program.

Wallace F. Bennett (1898–1993), Republican senator from Utah (during a Senate Subcommittee on Government Operations hearing, January 14, 1964)

World War II was the last government program that really worked.

George F. Will (1941–), opinion writer (speech at the annual meeting of the Association of American Publishers, White Sulphur Springs, West Virginia, April 28, 1975)

An oversize, overreaching federal government really is tearing us apart.

Glenn Reynolds (1960–), law school professor, University of Tennessee, opinion writer ("Election Results 2018: Forget the Blue Wave and Behold the Purple Puddle," USA Today, November 7, 2018)

GREAT MEN

Great men are the guideposts and landmarks in the state.

Edmund Burke (1729–1797), conservative British political thinker, statesman (in the House of Commons, London, April 19, 1774)

I have played some of the great men in history and I believe in the great man who does heroic deeds, even in these egalitarian times.

Charlton Heston (1923–2008), actor, National Rifle Association president (interview with Jani Allan, "Charlton Heston: Great Sport with a Line in Heroic Role Models," The Sunday Times, *June 17, 1990)*

The so-called Great Man theory of history might be overly simplistic, but history indisputably has its great men.

Rich Lowry (1968–), editor in chief, National Review *("Winston Churchill: The Man Who Saved Civilization,"* National Review Online, *December 29, 2017)*

HEARTLAND

Here, we are for America first, last, and all the time.

> *Robert R. McCormick (1880–1955), owner and
> publisher of the* Chicago Tribune *(Quoted in Felix
> Belair Jr., "M'Cormick Leans to Taft or Bricker,"*
> New York Times, *September 22, 1946)*

Foreignness is all around. Only in the heart of the heart of the country, namely the heart of the United States, can you avoid such a thing. In the center of an empire, you can think of your experience as universal. Outside the empire or on the fringes of the empire, you cannot.

> *Margaret Atwood (1939–), Canadian writer ("Margaret
> Atwood, The Art of Fiction,"* Paris Review, *winter 1990)*

I sometimes wonder if I would have been as successful had I not been born and raised in the heartland, in the middle of this country.

> *Rush Limbaugh (1951–), radio talk show host (The
> Rush Limbaugh Show, August 1, 2018. Rush grew up in
> southeastern Missouri.)*

HIGHER EDUCATION

One of the easiest things in the world is to assemble a list of hilarious courses offered in the colleges and universities of the United States.

Robert Maynard Hutchins (1899–1977), University of Chicago president (The Higher Learning in America [1961], "Preface")

— —

Administrators and staffers actually outnumber full-time faculty members at America's colleges and universities.

Benjamin Ginsberg (1947–), political science professor, Johns Hopkins University (The Fall of the Faculty: The Rise of the All-Administrative University and Why It Matters [2011], ch. 1)

— —

Actually, there hasn't been a single protestor at any of my last 30 speaking events (unless I was speaking at a university campus): But why bother with the facts?

Jordan Peterson (1962–), Canadian psychology professor, University of Toronto, motivational speaker (on Twitter, @JordanPeterson, May 30, 2018)

HISTORY

The disadvantage of men not knowing the past is that they do not know the present. History is a hill or high point of vantage, from which alone men see the town in which they live or the age in which they are living.

G. K. Chesterton (1874–1936), English journalist, critic, philosopher ("St. George in Our Times," Illustrated London News, *June 18, 1932)*

—•—

Ultimately, a real understanding of history means that we face NOTHING new under the sun.

James N. Mattis (1950–), U.S. Marine Corps general, secretary of defense under President Trump (email to a Marine colonel named Bill, November 20, 2003)

—•—

History is unpredictable. God writes straight with crooked lines.

John Lukacs (1924–2019), history professor, Chestnut Hill College ("Surrounded by Books," Chronicles: A Magazine of American Culture, *November 2, 2017)*

HOLLYWOOD

"The motion-picture business is the only business in the world in which you can make all the mistakes there are and still make money."

Raymond Chandler (1888–1959), detective fiction writer (movie mogul Jules Oppenheimer to private eye Philip Marlowe, in Chandler's novel The Little Sister *[1949], ch. 19)*

— —

Nobody abhors violence more than Hollywood, and nobody does more to glorify it.

Pat Sajak (1946–), host of Wheel of Fortune *(on Twitter, January 11, 2017)*

— —

Hollywood is a moral and intellectual pigsty, an asylum for the stupid, the corrupt, and the vocally shallow, who possess Thespian aptitudes or a saleable appearance and manner.

*Conrad Black (1944–), Canadian publisher, biographer (*Donald J. Trump: A President Like No Other *[2018], ch. 11)*

IMMIGRATION

The great social adventure of America is no longer the conquest of the wilderness but the absorption of fifty different peoples.

Walter Lippmann (1889–1974), journalist, political writer
(A Preface to Politics [1914], ch. 6)

Immigration without assimilation is invasion.

Bobby Jindal (1971–), Republican congressman and
governor from Louisiana (in the "undercard debate,"
August 6, 2015, during the 2016 campaign for the GOP
presidential nomination)

Rarely noticed in our era of the Beltway Behemoth is how sparse the Constitution is on the matter of central-government power over aliens.

Andrew McCarthy (1962–), former assistant United States
attorney, contributing editor, National Review *("The 14th*
Amendment Does Not Mandate Birthright Citizenship,"
National Review Online, *November 3, 2018)*

ISRAEL

I understand the Arabs wanting to wipe us out, but do they really expect us to cooperate?

Golda Meir (1898–1978), prime minister of Israel (quoted in Israel Shenker, "Golda Meir: Peace and Arab Acceptance Were Goals of Her 5 Years as Premier," New York Times, *December 9, 1978)*

———

It is the only nation on earth that inhabits the same land, bears the same name, speaks the same language, and worships the same God that it did 3,000 years ago.

Charles Krauthammer (1950–2018), opinion writer ("At Last, Zion: Israel and the Fate of the Jews," Weekly Standard, *May 11, 1998)*

———

Israel does what Israel has to do, just like the United States.

Charles Krauthammer (1950–2018), comment, circa 1981–1982, to a man who interrupted his meal at a Washington restaurant to complain about Israel's annexation of the Golan Heights (quoted in John Podhoretz, "Charles Krauthammer, 1950–2018: A Life Well Lived," Commentary.com, *June 21, 2018)*

ANDREW JACKSON

★★★

When you watch Trump, you need to recognize that he's one third Andrew Jackson in disruption, one third Theodore Roosevelt in sheer energy, and one third P. T. Barnum in selling all the time.

Newt Gingrich (1943—), former Republican congressman from Georgia, Speaker of the House (Interview with Susan Page, USA Today, *November 29, 2016)*

—　—

He was prickly, demanding and mercurial. He was no stranger to sexual scandal. His opponents regarded his presidency as unimaginable, until he beat them.

Michael Gerson (1964–), speechwriter for President George W. Bush, op-ed writer ("Trump Has Picked a Deeply Disturbing Hero," Washington Post, *March 16, 2017)*

—　—

It was during the Revolution that Jackson first confronted and defied an arrogant elite. Does that sound familiar to you? I wonder why they keep talking about Trump and Jackson, Jackson and Trump. Oh, I know the feeling, Andrew.

Donald Trump (1946–), real estate developer, television personality, president of the United States. Speaking at The Hermitage, Jackson's home in Nashville, March 23, 2017).

LEGAL SYSTEM

I must say that as a litigant I should dread a lawsuit beyond almost anything else short of sickness and death.

Learned Hand (1894–1961), federal judge ("The Deficiencies of Trials to Reach the Heart of the Matter," speech to the Bar Association of the City of New York, November 17, 1921)

—

The process is the punishment.

Malcolm Feeley (1942–), director of the Center for the Study of Law and Society, University of California, Berkeley (from the title of his book The Process Is the Punishment: Handling Cases in a Lower Criminal Court *[1979])*

—

"In a courtroom, whoever tells the best story wins."

Anthony Hopkins (1937–), actor (as the aging John Quincy Adams, in Amistad, *Steven Spielberg, dir., script by David Franzoni, released December 10, 1997)*

LIBERALISM

Liberalism is a mental disorder.

> *Michael Savage (1942–), radio talk show host (from the*
> *title of his book* Liberalism Is a Mental Disorder: Savage
> Solutions *[2005])*

— —

Left-liberals have no sense of humour.

> *James Delingpole (1955-), English novelist, opinion*
> *writer, Brexit supporter ("You Know It Makes Sense." The*
> *Spectator, April 28, 2009)*

— —

Liberals don't care what you do as long as it's compulsory.

> *M. Stanton Evans (1934–2016), writer and editor (quoted*
> *in "The Wit and Wisdom of M. Stanton Evans," Chicago*
> *Lampoon, December 29, 2010)*

— —

The free lunch is the essence of modern liberalism.

> *Charles Krauthammer (1950–2018), opinion writer*
> *("Obamacare Laid Bare," Washington Post,*
> *November 1, 2013)*

LIBERTY

You must remember, my fellow-citizens, that eternal vigilance by the people is the price of liberty, and that you must pay the price if you wish to secure the blessing.

> *Andrew Jackson (1767–1845), Tennessee congressman and senator, president of the United States (farewell address as president, March 14, 1837)*

Liberty is not a means to a higher political end. It is itself the highest political end.

> *John Dalberg-Acton, 1st Baron Acton (1834–1902), English historian and politician (in his speech "The History of Freedom in Antiquity," February 26, 1877)*

Freedom is a luxury that can be afforded only by the good society. When civic virtue diminishes, freedom will inevitably diminish as well.

> *Antonin Scalia (1936–2016), associate Supreme Court justice (commencement address, Langley High School, Langley, Virginia, June 21, 1994)*

ABRAHAM LINCOLN

God gave us Lincoln and Liberty; let us fight for both.

Attributed to Ulysses S. Grant (1822–1885), Union Army commanding general in the Civil War, president of the United States (February 22, 1863, before the start of the Vicksburg Campaign, quoted in Edward Deering Mansfield, A Popular and Authentic Life of Ulysses S. Grant *[1868], ch. 15)*

Hemingway claimed that all modern American novels are the offspring of *Huckleberry Finn*. It is no greater exaggeration to say that all modern political prose descends from the Gettysburg Address.

Garry Wills (1934–), author, former National Review *contributor ("The Words That Remade America,"* The Atlantic, *June 1992)*

People admire Washington but they love Lincoln.

Thomas J. Craughwell (1956–2018), nonfiction writer (quoted in Don Babwin, "Book Details Plot to Steal Abe's Body," Washington Post, *May 7, 2007)*

MEN AND WOMEN

★★★

In politics, if you want anything said, ask a man; if you want anything done, ask a woman.

> *Margaret Thatcher (1925–2013), British prime minister (speech at the Royal Albert Hall, London, May 20, 1965)*

— ◆ —

Guess what—women are different than men! When will feminism wake up to this basic reality?

> *Camille Paglia (1947–), humanities professor, University of the Arts, Philadelphia (quoted in David Daley, "Camille Paglia Takes on Jon Stewart, Trump, Sanders," Salon.com, July 29, 2015)*

— ◆ —

The guy who thinks he's smarter than his wife has no idea how truly smart she is.

> *Rush Limbaugh (1951–), talk show host (repeating a favorite saying on* The Rush Limbaugh Show, *January 5, 2018)*

THE MIDDLE EAST

★ ★ ★

The core of the conflicts in the Middle East is the battle between modernity and early primitive medievalism.

> *Benjamin Netanyahu (1949–), prime minister of Israel*
> *(quoted in Jonah Goldberg, "Netanyahu's Framing of*
> *Middle East Situation Is Spot-on," National Review Online,*
> *November 13, 2015)*

━ ━

Saying you don't want to enter every potential war in the Middle East doesn't make you an isolationist; it makes you wise.

> *Nigel Farage (1964–), member of the European Parliament,*
> *founder of the Brexit political party (quoted in Tara John,*
> *"Nigel Farage Claims Donald Trump's Election Win as*
> *'Brexit Times Three,'" Time.com, November 9, 2016)*

━ ━

American leaders are learning that which other great powers have learned about the Mideast throughout history: there are no good options there. Dealing in that region is a lose-lose proposition.

> *Brandon J. Weichert (1988–), geopolitical analyst ("Does*
> *Washington Want to Lose Little or Bigly in the Mideast?,"*
> *The American Spectator, October 13, 2018)*

Minimum Wage

I don't know of a single economist who disagrees that when you raise the minimum wage, you kill jobs for the poor.

Newt Gingrich (1943–), Republican congressman from Georgia, Speaker of the House (to one of his constituents, mid-June 1999. Quoted in David Beers, "Master of Disaster," Mother Jones, October 1999.)

The real minimum wage is always zero, regardless of the laws, and that is the wage that many workers receive in the wake of creation or escalation of a government-mandated minimum wage, because they either lose their jobs or fail to find jobs when they enter the work force.

Thomas Sowell (1930–), economist, Hoover Institution senior fellow (Basic Economics: A Common Sense Guide to the Economy (2007), in the section, "Minimum Wage Laws")

MODERATE REPUBLICAN

★ ★ ★

Dime Store New Deal.

> *Barry Goldwater (1909–1998), Arizona senator, 1964*
> *Republican presidential nominee (title of a Senate speech,*
> *May 5, 1960, slamming the "modern Republicanism" of the*
> *Eisenhower administration, which, Goldwater said, had*
> *been seduced by the "siren song of socialism")*

— ◆ —

I resist the word "moderate" because it is a base-stealing word for the benefit of GOP liberals.

> *William F. Buckley Jr. (1925–2008),* National Review *editor*
> *in chief, columnist, talk show host, novelist ("On the Right,"*
> *Buckley's syndicated column, as published in the* Syracuse
> Post-Standard, *March 21, 1967)*

— ◆ —

"Moderate Republican" is simply how the blabocracy flatters Republicans who vote with the Democrats. If it weren't so conspicuous, the *New York Times* would start referring to "nice Republicans" and "mean Republicans."

> *Ann Coulter (1961–), writer, commentator (*Slander:
> Liberal Lies About the American Right *[2002])*

THE MUELLER REPORT

★★★

If Mueller felt it so necessary to include in his report any material he swept up as he vacuumed around, why not at least suggest that the FBI Director and members of DOJ did not honestly inform a FISA court of the true nature of the evidence for their writ—given the centrality of surveilled conversations within the Mueller report?

Victor Davis Hanson (1953–), military historian, classics professor, Hoover Institution senior fellow ("Inquisitio Requiescat in Pace," National Review Online, *April 18, 2019)*

—•—

"Donald Trump attempted to obstruct our effort to throw him out of office," is how this report should read.

*Rush Limbaugh (1951–), talk show host (*The Rush Limbaugh Show, *April 18, 2019)*

—•—

If you find yourself blaming President Trump for almost-sort-of-maybe intending to obstruct a witch hunt you have a mental health crisis not a political opinion.

Scott Adams (1957–), creator of the comic strip Dilbert *(on Twitter, @ScottAdamsSays, April 18, 2019)*

Multiculturalism

The great thing about multiculturalism is it doesn't involve knowing anything about other cultures…It's a quintessential piece of progressive humbug.

Mark Steyn (1959–), Canadian-born political and pop culture writer ("It's the Demography, Stupid," The New Criterion, January 2006)

What "multiculturalism" boils down to is that you can praise any culture in the world except Western culture—and you cannot blame any culture in the world except Western culture.

Thomas Sowell (1930–), economist, Hoover Institution Senior Fellow ("Random Thoughts," TownHall.com, September 12, 2012)

Trump's culture war is fundamentally the people versus the elite, national sovereignty versus cosmopolitanism and patriotism versus multiculturalism.

Rich Lowry (1968–), editor in chief, National Review *("How Trump Is Remaking the 'Culture War,'" New York Post, January 23, 2017)*

NATIONALISM

I'm not a white nationalist. I'm a nationalist. I'm an economic nationalist.

> *Steve Bannon (1953–), co-founder, Breitbart News, 2016 campaign advisor to Donald Trump (interview with Michael Wolff, "Ringside with Steve Bannon at Trump Tower,"* Hollywood Reporter, *November 18, 2016)*

— • —

One of the reasons many conservatives have decided to get drunk on nationalism is that so many liberals have cut patriotism from their diets.

> *Jonah Goldberg (1969–), opinion writer,* National Review Online *editor-at-large ("Being Inspired by U.S. Achievements Shouldn't Be Partisan,"* National Review Online, *September 5, 2018)*

— • —

Nationalists can talk to one another; with internationalists, oddly enough, talking doesn't work so well.

> *Michel Houellebecq (1956–), French writer ("Donald Trump Is a Good President: One Foreigner's Perspective,"* Harper's, *January 2019)*

NATO

NATO exists for three reasons—to keep the Russians out, the Americans in, and the Germans down.

> *Attributed to Lionel "Pug" Ismay (1887–1965), military aide to Winston Churchill, first secretary general of NATO (quoted in Peter Hennessy,* Never Again: Britain, 1945–1951 *[1992])*

NATO is and always has been simply a defensive alliance shielding those of like mind and interest.

> *John Bolton (1948–), national security advisor to President Trump ("NATO Is Still the Answer,"* The Weekly Standard, *May 5, 2014)*

There has been no substantial thought about what NATO is for since the Berlin Wall came down. Trump is right about members not paying their way.

> *Nigel Farage (1964–), member of the European Parliament, founder of the Brexit political party (quoted in Jon Sharman, "Ex-Ukip Leader Wants to Build Peace in Middle East,"* The Independent, *December 9, 2016)*

Neo-Conservative

I define a neo-conservative as a liberal who has been mugged by reality.

> *Irving Kristol (1920–2009), conservative intellectual, father of William Kristol ("The New American Conservatism: An Interview with Irving Kristol," State Legislatures, November–December 1980)*

The neoconservatives maintain a sense of aristocratic entitlement to rule despite having killed almost everything they touched. It is their combination of titanic hubris and priggish moralism that is behind their aggressive advocacy of endless foreign wars and meddling in the internal affairs of other countries.

> *Chris Buskirk (1969–), publisher and editor of AmericanGreatness.com, opinion writer, publius fellow at the Claremont Institute ("Death of The Weekly Standard Signals Rebirth of the Right," AmericanGreatness.com, December 17, 2018)*

BARACK OBAMA

Barack Obama is an immensely talented man whose talents have been largely devoted to crafting, and chronicling, his own life. Not things. Not ideas. Not institutions. But himself.

> *Charles Krauthammer (1950–2018), opinion writer ("The Perfect Stranger,"* Washington Post, *August 21, 2008)*

So I shamelessly say, no, I want him to fail, if his agenda is a far-left collectivism, some people say socialism, as a conservative...why would I want socialism to succeed?

> *Rush Limbaugh (1951–), talk show host (reply when asked if he wished Barack Obama well as president, on the Fox News program* Hannity's America, *January 22, 2009)*

President Obama was not friendly to the press, but the press was very friendly to President Obama.

> *Jake Tapper (1969–), CNN news anchor (interview with Taffy Brodesser-Akner, "The Realest Face in 'Fake News,'"* GQ, *May 2017)*

OBSCENITY

Sex and obscenity are not synonymous. Obscene material is material which deals with sex in a manner appealing to prurient interest.

William J. Brennan (1906–1997), associate Supreme Court justice (Roth v. United States, *decided June 24, 1957)*

—●—

I know it when I see it.

Potter Stewart (1915–1985), associate Supreme Court justice (concurring opinion, Jacobellis v. Ohio, *decided June 22, 1964, referring to hard-core pornography)*

—●—

In no state of the Union two centuries ago, would foul speech or publication have been tolerated by the public authorities—notwithstanding provisions in state constitutions for freedom of speech and press.

Russell Kirk (1918–1994), political and social theorist (Rights and Duties: Reflections on Our Conservative Constitution *[1997], ch. 15)*

Ordinary Americans

Who listens to me? The answer is obvious: All across the fruited plain, ordinary Americans of every walk of life listen. You know who you are—you are the ones who have the courage to face and believe the truth. You are the people who make the country work.

*Rush Limbaugh (1951–), talk show host (*See, I Told You So *[1993], ch. 2)*

The average guy is fairly smart, if you give him the ability to make decisions for himself. That's the whole premise of America, and that's why America has prospered, and it prospers because if the average guy can get information, he can make his own decisions.

Tom Clancy (1947–2013), author of thriller novels (on Larry King Weekend, *August 27, 2000)*

PATRIOTISM

That we can die but once to serve our Country!

Joseph Addison (1672–1719), English man of letters (Cato [1713], act IV, scene 2, spoken by Cato the Elder, inspired by the corpse of his heroic son)

— ▪ —

In offering to you, my countrymen, these counsels of an old and affectionate friend…to moderate the fury of party spirit, to warn against the mischiefs of foreign intrigue, to guard against the impostures of pretended patriotism.

George Washington (1732–1799), commander, American forces in the Revolution, president of the United States (farewell address as president, published September 19, 1796)

— ▪ —

My fellow Americans: ask not what your country can do for you—ask what you can do for your country.

John F. Kennedy (1917–1963), Massachusetts senator, president of the United States (inaugural address, January 20, 1961)

PEACE

Wars are, of course, to be avoided; but they are far better than certain kinds of peace.

> *Ulysses S. Grant (1822–1885), Union Army commanding general in the Civil War, president of the United States (speech in London, quoted in Stephen Merrill Allen, Memorial Life of Gen. Ulysses S. Grant [1889], ch. 22. Grant visited England in 1877.)*

Although a soldier by profession, I have never felt any sort of fondness for war, and I have never advocated it, except as a means of peace.

> *Theodore Roosevelt (1858–1919), governor of New York, vice president and president of the United States (Thomas Hart Benton [1897], ch. 12)*

Peace Through Strength.

> *Bernard Baruch (1870–1965), financier, advisor to President Franklin Roosevelt (title of a book by Baruch published in 1952)*

POLITICAL CORRECTNESS

Political correctness is tyranny with manners.

> *Charlton Heston (1923–2008), actor, National Rifle Association president (speech at Harvard Law School, February 16, 1999)*

Political correctness has done great damage to the study and appreciation of art, but "this too shall pass." Ars longa, PC brevis.

> *Roger Kimball (1953–), editor, author, and publisher,* The New Criterion *(Q&A with John J. Miller, "The Rape of the Masters,"* National Review Online, *July 20, 2004)*

We don't need to be politically correct. We need to be morally right.

> *Jeanine Pirro (1951–), former district attorney, author, and host of the Fox News show* Justice with Judge Jeanine *(speaking at the ACT for America conference in Washington, D.C., Sept. 11, 2014)*

Political correctness has become synonymous with either cowardice or careerism—or both.

> *Victor Davis Hanson (1953–), military historian, classics professor, Hoover Institution senior fellow ("The Great Regression,"* National Review Online, *August 16, 2016)*

POLITICIANS

★★★

I think politicians, like diapers, should be changed regularly.

*Betty Carpenter (1929–2012), co-owner, Busy B's Restaurant
& Bar, Fort Thomas, Kentucky (comment made during her
campaign for Fort Thomas City Council, quoted in "Special
Report: Election Guide,"* Cincinnati Enquirer,
October 25, 1987)

A gaffe is when a politician tells the truth—some obvious truth he isn't supposed to say.

*Michael Kinsley (1951–), journalist, editor ("Commentary:
The Gaffer Speaks,"* The Times *of London, April 23, 1988)*

Politicians will always disappoint you.

*William Rusher (1923–2011), attorney, columnist, and
publisher of* National Review *(quoted in Jonah Goldberg,
"Living in the Real World: Everyone Has to Do It, Including
Conservatives,"* National Review, *March 27, 2006)*

POLITICS

Politics is said to be the second oldest profession. I have come to realize that it bears a very close resemblance to the first.

> *Ronald Reagan (1911–2004), actor, governor of California,*
> *president of the United States (quoted in George Skelton,*
> *"Reagan Slaps Politics in Talk for GOP Candidate*
> *McLennan," Los Angeles Times, October 25, 1974)*

— ∙ —

Politics is tribalism for most people.

> *Kevin D. Williamson (1972–), libertarian opinion writer*
> *("Progressives without Power," National Review Online,*
> *November 26, 2016)*

— ∙ —

The first law of contemporary politics: There is no such thing as rock bottom.

> *George F. Will (1941–), opinion writer ("There's No Such*
> *Thing as Rock Bottom," Washington Post,*
> *September 27, 2018)*

Popular Culture

I'm not a fundamentalist, saying there's no difference between Homer and Walt Disney. But Mickey Mouse can be perfect in the sense that a Japanese haiku is.

> *Umberto Eco (1932–2016), Italian critic and fiction writer (quoted in Maya Jaggi, "Signs of the Times," The Guardian, October 12, 2002)*

—-—

These days, popular culture is democracy.

> *Norah Vincent (1968—), author ("Both Sides Now," New York Times Book Review, February 18, 2007)*

—-—

I don't really like the expression "popular culture." It's just "culture" now: there is no other. "High culture" is high mainly in the sense we keep it in the attic and dust it off and bring it downstairs every now and then.

> *Mark Steyn (1959–), Canadian-born political and pop culture writer ("Twenty Years Ago Today," The New Criterion, November 2007)*

ALL POWER

TO THE

POWERFUL

POWER

Power always thinks it has a great soul and vast views, beyond the comprehension of the weak.

> *John Adams (1735–1826), co-author, Declaration of Independence, president of the United States (letter to Thomas Jefferson, February 2, 1816)*

The possession of great power necessarily implies great responsibility.

> *William Lamb, 2nd Viscount Melbourne (1779–1848), British prime minister (in Parliament, July 12, 1817)*

Power tends to corrupt, and absolute power corrupts absolutely. Great men are almost always bad men, even when they exercise influence and not authority, still more when you superadd the tendency or the certainty of corruption by authority.

> *John Dalberg-Acton, 1st Baron Acton (1834–1902), English historian and politician (letter to Bishop Mandell Creighton, April 5, 1887)*

PRESIDENCY

There have been times in this office when I wondered how you could do the job if you hadn't been an actor.

Ronald Reagan (1911–2004), actor, governor of California, president of the United States (interview with David Brinkley, aired on ABC News, *December 22, 1988)*

In our brief national history we have shot four of our presidents, worried five of them to death, impeached one and hounded another out of office. And when all else fails, we hold an election and assassinate their character.

P. J. O'Rourke (1947–), humorist, essayist, novelist (A Parliament of Whores [1991], "The President")

The presidency is no longer about what we used to conventionally understand as politics. Instead, the president has become a totem, an object of popular veneration who supposedly embodies who we are.

Kevin D. Williamson (1972–), libertarian opinion writer ("The Snob Party," National Review Online, *November 26, 2018)*

Pro-Life

I've noticed that everybody that is for abortion has already been born.

> *Ronald Reagan (1911–2004), actor, governor of California, president of the United States (in his September 21, 1980, debate in Baltimore against Independent presidential candidate John Anderson, which Jimmy Carter refused to attend)*

The freedom women were supposed to have found in the Sixties largely boiled down to easy contraception and abortion: things to make life easier for men, in fact.

> *Julie Burchill (1959–), English journalist, author (Damaged Gods: Cults and Heroes Reappraised [1986], "Born Again Cows")*

You can't have Liberty and the Pursuit of Happiness if you don't have Life.

> *Ben Carson (1951–), neurosurgeon, Johns Hopkins Hospital, secretary of Housing and Urban Development in the Trump administration (to Megyn Kelly on the Fox News Channel program The Kelly File, July 28, 2015)*

PUBLIC OPINION

Public opinion sets bounds to every government, and is the real sovereign in every free one.

> *James Madison (1751–1836), secretary of state, president of the United States ("Public Opinion," National Gazette, December 19, 1791)*

It is a besetting vice of democracies to substitute public opinion for law. This is the usual form in which masses of men exhibit their tyranny.

> *James Fenimore Cooper (1789–1851), writer, U.S. Consul at Lyon, France (The American Democrat, or Hints on the Social and Civic Relations of the United States of America [1838], "On the Disadvantages of a Democracy")*

The nobility of politics, when it is noble, often consists in prudent maneuvering and persuading until an issue is, in terms of public opinion, ripe.

> *George F. Will (1941–), opinion writer ("Gore's Warming to A Candidacy?" Washington Post, June 11, 2006)*

RACISM

The new grammar of race is constructed in a way that George Orwell would have appreciated, because its rules make some ideas impossible to express—unless, of course, one wants to be called a racist.

Stephen L. Carter (1954–), African-American law professor, Yale University (Reflections of an Affirmative Action Baby [1992], ch. 8)

— —

Honesty has itself been routinely cast as racist.

Harry Stein (1948–), writer and humorist (No Matter What…They'll Call This Book Racist: How our Fear of Talking Honestly About Race Hurts Us All [2012], "Introduction")

— —

Today the word *racist* is used the way *communist* was used in the early 1950s.

Michael Savage (1942–), radio talk show host (Stop Mass Hysteria: America's Insanity from the Salem Witch Trials to the Trump Witch Hunt [2018], ch. 1)

— —

You think racism can control me? Oh, *that don't stop me,* that's an invisible wall!

Kanye West (1977–), rapper, songwriter, entrepreneur (in the Oval Office with President Trump, October 11, 2018)

RONALD REAGAN

★★★

The Rembrandt of American conservatism.

> *James L. Buckley (1923–), New York senator, federal judge,*
> *brother of William F. Buckley (introducing Reagan at a*
> *conservative conference in Washington, D.C.,*
> *February 25, 1975)*

— —

One of Clare Boothe Luce's sharper epigrams was: A great man is one sentence. Well, I will sum up the achievements of President Reagan in a sentence too: Ronald Reagan won the Cold War without firing a shot.

> *Margaret Thatcher (1925–2013), British prime minister*
> *(Clare Boothe Luce Lecture, Heritage Foundation,*
> *Washington, D.C., September 23, 1991)*

— —

I remember in '79, '80, Democrats said, "You know, Reagan's an actor." Like voters don't know that. There's a smugness to that attitude that causes the voting public to go, "We're smarter than that."

> *Lorne Michaels (1944–), creator of the NBC television*
> *program* Saturday Night Live *(Maureen Dowd, "Is the 2016*
> *Election Beyond Satire? Ask Lorne Michaels," New York*
> *Times Magazine, February 9, 2016)*

RELIGION

★★★

Of all the dispositions and habits which lead to political prosperity, religion and morality are indispensable supports....And let us with caution indulge the supposition that morality can be maintained without religion.

George Washington (1732–1799), commander, American forces in the Revolution, first president of the United States (farewell address as president, published September 19, 1796)

——

It is quite clear that the Founding Fathers wanted the right of religious observation and would never have accepted a government that was driving God out of the public square.

Newt Gingrich (1943–), Republican congressman from Georgia, Speaker of the House (quoted in Sabrina Arena Ferrisi, "Religion in the Public Square," Legatus Magazine, *July 1, 2010)*

——

Sneering at religion is juvenile, symptomatic of a stunted imagination.

*Camille Paglia (1947–), humanities professor, University of the Arts, Philadelphia (*Glittering Images: A Journey Through Art from Egypt to Star Wars *[2012], "Introduction")*

REPUBLICAN PARTY

★★★

Thou shalt not speak ill of any Republican.

Gaylord B. Parkinson II (1918–2010), chair, California Republican State Central Committee ("Parkinson's Eleventh Commandment," delivered at a committee meeting in San Francisco, quoted the next day in Carl Greenberg, "Public Fight, Bad Politics," Los Angeles Times, *September 26, 1965)*

———

Republicans buy sneakers, too.

Michael Jordan (1963–), guard and forward, Chicago Bulls and Washington Wizards (defending his decision not to endorse a black candidate running against Republican senator Jesse Helms in North Carolina in 1990, quoted in David Halberstam, Playing for Keeps: Michael Jordan and the World He Made *[1999], ch. 28)*

———

I'm a Christian, a conservative, and a Republican, in that order.

Mike Pence (1959–), vice president of the United States (acceptance speech as Republican vice presidential nominee, Cleveland, Ohio, July 21, 2016)

REPUBLICANS VS. DEMOCRATS

There are a lot of bad Republicans; there are no good Democrats.

Ann Coulter (1961–), writer, commentator (on the C-SPAN program Booknotes *with Brian Lamb, August 11, 2002)*

— —

You know, Democrats and Republicans are interesting because Republicans really laugh at themselves more.

Jay Leno (1950–), comedian (on Meet the Press, *April 22, 2012)*

— —

Democrats find nothing good in any conservative, ever, until he is safely retired or dead. Every Republican president is the worst president ever, until the next one.

Kyle Smith (1966–), National Review critic-at-large ("Impeachment Is Not Going to Happen." National Review Online, August 23, 2018)

THEODORE ROOSEVELT

I told William McKinley it was a mistake to nominate that wild man in Philadelphia. I asked him if he realized what would happen if he should die. Now look, that damned cowboy is President of the United States!

> *Mark Hanna (1837–1904), advisor to President McKinley*
> *(to his friend H. H. Kohlsaat, publisher of the* Chicago
> Record-Herald, *September 16, 1901, the day after McKinley*
> *was assassinated and Roosevelt succeeded him as president,*
> *quoted in Kohlsaat's book,* From McKinley to Harding
> *[1923], ch. 21)*

Roosevelt started from the premise that the United States was a power like any other, not a singular incarnation of virtue. If its interests collided with those of other countries, America had the obligation to draw on its strength to prevail.

> *Henry Kissinger (1923–), professor of government, Harvard*
> *University, secretary of state under Presidents Nixon and*
> *Ford (*Diplomacy *[1994], ch. 2)*

Second Amendment

You know why there's a Second Amendment? In case the government fails to follow the first one.

> *Rush Limbaugh (1951–), radio talk show host (*The Rush Limbaugh Show, *August 17, 1993)*

——

The purpose of the right to bear arms is twofold; to allow individuals to protect themselves and their families, and to ensure a body of armed citizenry from which a militia could be drawn, whether that militia's role was to protect the nation, or to protect the people from a tyrannical government.

> *Glenn Reynolds (1960–), law school professor, University of Tennessee, blogger, columnist ("A Critical Guide to the Second Amendment," *Tennessee Law Review, *spring 1995)*

——

We got to remember, the Second Amendment is about freedom.

> *Jim Jordan (1964—), Republican congressman from Ohio (On *Fox News Sunday, *with John Roberts, January 6, 2013)*

SOCIALISM

Socialism is the philosophy of failure, the creed of ignorance, and the gospel of envy.

> *Winston Churchill (1874–1965), British statesman (speech in Perth, Scotland, May 28, 1948)*

— —

If you think health care is expensive now, wait until you see what it costs when it is free.

> *P. J. O'Rourke (1947–), humorist, essayist, novelist (speech to the Cato Institute, Washington, D.C., May 6, 1993)*

— —

Socialism in general has a record of failure so blatant that only an intellectual could ignore or evade it.

> *Thomas Sowell (1930–), economist, Hoover Institution senior fellow ("The Survival of the Left," Forbes, September 8, 1997)*

SUPREME COURT

★ ★ ★

When the Court moved to Washington in 1800, it was provided with no books, which probably accounts for the high quality of early opinions.

> *Robert H. Jackson (1892–1954), associate Supreme Court justice (*The Supreme Court in the American System of Government *[1955], based on drafts of three lectures Jackson planned to deliver at Harvard University in 1955)*

— —

Let me put this bluntly—every time the Supreme Court meets in secret conference, it sits as a constitutional convention, rewriting the Constitution at will.

> *Mark Levin (1957–), talk show host ("The Court,"* National Review Online, *June 25, 2008)*

— —

Our political commentary talks about the Supreme Court like they are people wearing red and blue jerseys. That's a really dangerous thing.

> *Ben Sasse (1961–), Republican senator from Nebraska (during the Senate hearing on Judge Brett Kavanaugh's nomination to the Supreme Court, September 4, 2018)*

TAXES

★★★

We live in the only country in the world where it takes more brains to figure out your income tax than it does to earn the income.

Ronald Reagan (1911–2004), actor, governor of California, president of the United States (on The Tonight Show Starring Johnny Carson, *March 13, 1975)*

— —

Tax cuts are like sex; when they are good, they are very, very good. And when they are bad, they are still pretty good.

M. Stanton Evans (1934–2016), writer and editor, National Review, *editorial page editor,* Indianapolis News *("The Wit and Wisdom of M. Stanton Evans,"* Chicago Lampoon, *December 29, 2010)*

— —

Government spending is taxation pure and simple. There's no tooth fairy working in the Treasury any longer. Whenever the government spends they take it from someone else.

Arthur Laffer (1940–), economic advisor to President Ronald Reagan (interview with Mehdi Hasan, Head to Head *[AlJazeera.com], April 6, 2015.*

Margaret Thatcher

★★★

The Iron Lady.

> *The Soviet Army newspaper* Red Star *pinned this sobriquet on Mrs. Thatcher following a speech harshly critical of the Soviet Union she gave on January 19, 1976 ("Iron Lady" is a play on "Iron Duke," the nickname of the Duke of Wellington, who defeated Napoleon at Waterloo)*

— —

To those waiting with bated breath for that favorite media catchphrase, the "U" turn, I have only one thing to say. "You turn if you want to. The lady's not for turning."

> *Margaret Thatcher (1925–2013), British prime minister (Conservative Party Conference in Brighton, England, October 10, 1980)*

— —

Even if Reagan was all fame and nothing else, for now that was enough. There was no man in America to match him. The only man to match him was in Britain, and she was a woman. Margaret Thatcher carried on with all the confidence of Winston Churchill minus the cigar, drumming up memories of a Britain with a seat at the top table.

> *Clive James (1939–2019), British writer (Fame in the 20th Century [1993], ch. 8)*

TOLERANCE

Complete moral tolerance is possible only when men have become completely indifferent to each other—that is to say, when society is at an end.

James Fitzjames Stephen (1829–1894), English jurist
(Liberty, Fraternity, Equality [1873], ch. 4)

We live in a world of intolerance masked as tolerance.

Rush Limbaugh (1951–), radio talk show host (The Rush
Limbaugh Show, March 7, 2012)

Tolerance is the totem of our age, a bumper sticker of virtue. Yet hidden in its many meanings is the doublespeak of defining what will be taboo. It is now considered tolerant to demand silence from nonconformists.

Chris Uhlmann (1960–), Australian journalist ("There
Was a Time When Journalists Backed Free Speech," The
Weekend Australian, February 20, 2016)

TOTALITARIANISM

Thought control is a copyright of totalitarianism, and we have no claim to it. It is not the function of the government to keep the citizen from falling into error; it is the function of the citizen to keep the government from falling into error.

*Robert H. Jackson (1892–1954), associate Supreme Court justice (*American Communications Association v. Douds, *decided May 8, 1950)*

—

The all-seeing eye of a totalitarian regime is usually the watchful eye of the next-door neighbor.

*Eric Hoffer (18981–983), German-born longshoreman, self-taught philosopher ("Thoughts on the Brotherhood of Men," *New York Times Magazine, *February 15, 1959)*

—

Liberalism…is totalitarian in nature. It is an effort to control everybody, or as many people as possible. It's based on the assumption that most people are blithering idiots and haven't the ability to lead responsible lives on their own.

*Rush Limbaugh (1951––), talk show host (*The Rush Limbaugh Show, *February 29, 2008)*

TRADITION

Tradition lives because young people come along who catch its romance and add new glories to it.

Michael Novak (1933–2017), Catholic philosopher, ambassador to the United Nations Commission on Human Rights ("Public Arguments: October 7, 1571—The Battle of Lepanto," Crisis, October 1994)

One thing that conservatives overlook in their worldview is tradition. We favor limited government, free enterprise, the social issues, a strong defense, but as to the basic theme of tradition we slide over it.

R. Emmett Tyrrell Jr. (1943–), editor in chief, The American Spectator ("The State of Our Tradition," The American Spectator, May 24, 2016)

Tradition is rooted in manners and custom, and customs weigh against the excesses of personal freedom. Conservatives know there will always be tensions between the two.

R. Emmett Tyrrell Jr. ("At the Bullfights, Olé," American Spectator, May 22, 2019)

DONALD TRUMP

The media did not make Donald Trump, and they can't destroy him.

Rush Limbaugh (1951–), talk show host (interview with Chris Wallace, Fox News Sunday, *February 19, 2017)*

＊

Donald Trump came to us at a time when we needed his tough talk and unvarnished perspective.

Jeanine Pirro (1951–), former district attorney, author, and host of the Fox News show Justice with Judge Jeanine *(Liars, Leakers, and Liberals: The Case Against the Anti-Trump Conspiracy [2018], ch. 1)*

＊

I don't know about you, but I cannot keep up with this President and yet I'm still not tired of winning.

Clarice Feldman (1941–), opinion writer and blogger ("Is Trump the Most Fun President Ever?," AmericanThinker .com, *July 1, 2018)*

＊

Trump is on his hero's journey right now.

Kanye West (1977–), rapper, songwriter, entrepreneur (in the Oval Office with President Trump, October 11, 2018)

TYRANNY

The tyranny of a multitude is a multiplied tyranny.

> *Edmund Burke (1729–1797), conservative British political thinker, statesman (A Letter from Mr. Burke: To a Member of the National Assembly; in Answer to Some Objections to His Book on French Affairs [1791], January 19, 1791)*

— —

I have sworn upon the altar of God eternal hostility against every form of tyranny over the mind of man.

> *Thomas Jefferson (1743–1826), co-author, Declaration of Independence, president of the United States, founder of the University of Virginia (Letter to Benjamin Rush, September 23, 1800)*

— —

When the people fear the government, there is tyranny. When the government fears the people, there is liberty.

> *John Basil Barnhill (1864–1929), politician, debater on the Chautauqua circuit ("Indictment of Socialism No. 3," in Barnhill-Tichenor Debate on Socialism, As It Appeared in the National Rip-Saw [1914])*

UNITED NATIONS

There *is no* United Nations. There is an international community that occasionally can be led by the only real power left in the world, and that's the United States, when it suits our interests, and when we can get others to go along.

John Bolton (1948–), national security advisor to President Trump (at the Global Structures Convocation hosted by the World Federalist Association, New York, February 3, 1994)

— —

The UN is worse than disaster. The UN creates conflicts. Look at the disgraceful UN Human Rights Council. It transmits norms which are harmful, anti-liberty, and anti-Semitic among other things. The world would be better off in its absence.

Charles Krauthammer (1950–2018), opinion writer (quoted in "Obama Is Average," Der Spiegel, online October 26, 2009)

VIETNAM WAR

The great immorality of the Vietnam War was for our government to be asking young men to give up their lives in that war when the government had no intention of winning it.

> *Ronald Reagan (1911–2004), actor, governor of California, president of the United States (interview at the White House, September 12, 1988, for the PBS documentary* John Wayne: Standing Tall)

— —

Vietnam was really an idealistic thing to stop the spread of communism, which, incidentally, it did. It was a pretty costly way to do it, but it achieved its goal.

> *Tom Wolfe (1931–2018), writer (quoted in Tim Adams, "Dances with Wolfe,"* The Guardian, *January 20, 2008)*

— —

The simple truth is the American establishment lost the war in Vietnam because it lacked the will to win it.

> *Patrick J. Buchanan (1938–), advisor to Presidents Nixon, Ford, and Reagan, pundit, two-time candidate for president (*Nixon's White House Wars *[2017], ch. 20)*

Virtue Signaling

A lot of what happens on Facebook, as with Twitter, is "virtue signalling"—showing off how right on you are.

Helen Lewis (1983–), English journalist ("The Echo Chamber of Social Media Is Luring the Left into Cosy Delusion and Dangerous Insularity," New Statesman, *July 22, 2015)*

Competitive "virtue signaling" has become the way of political life in America.

Angelo Codevilla (1943–), professor emeritus, Pardee School of Global Studies, Boston University ("Diplomacy 101 Versus Politics Writ Small," AmericanGreatness.com, *July 17, 2018)*

Over the last twenty years, marquee journalists saw themselves as wannabe celebrities who were to make news, not to report it, to massage stories in such a fashion to serve their social justice agendas, and to virtue signal their superior morality.

Victor Davis Hanson (1953—), military historian, classics professor, Hoover Institution senior fellow ("Journalism Is Dead—Long Live the Media!," AmericanGreatness.com, *May 12, 2019)*

WAR

Victory or death.

> *George Washington (1732–1799), commander, American*
> *forces in the Revolution, president of the United States*
> *(Washington's watchword for his bold attack on the Hessian*
> *garrison at Trenton, Christmas Day, 1776)*

Surrender is not an option if you plan to win a war. Victory at all costs, victory in spite of all terror, victory however long and hard the road may be; for without victory there is no survival.

> *Winston Churchill (1874–1965), British statesman (in the*
> *House of Commons during the Battle of Britain,*
> *May 13, 1940)*

No war is over until the enemy says it's over. We may think it over, we may declare it over, but in fact, the enemy gets a vote.

> *James N. Mattis (1950–), U.S. Marine Corps general,*
> *secretary of defense under President Trump (keynote speech*
> *at a foreign policy conference, Washington, D.C.,*
> *February 12, 2009)*

GEORGE WASHINGTON

To the memory of the Man, first in war, first in peace, and first in the hearts of his countrymen.

Henry "Light-Horse Harry" Lee (1756–1818), Revolutionary War officer, Virginia governor and congressman ("Eulogy on Washington," delivered December 26, 1799, and published in Resolutions Presented to the United States' House of Representatives, on the Death of Washington, December, 1799)

He was, indeed, in every sense of the words, a wise, a good, & a great man.

Thomas Jefferson (1743–1826), co-author, Declaration of Independence, president of the United States, founder of the University of Virginia (letter to Dr. Walter Jones, January 2, 1814)

History has hardly a stronger case of an indispensable man.

*Goldwin Smith (1823–1910), Canadian historian (*The United States: An Outline of Political History, 1492–1871 *[1893], ch. 2)*

Welcome to
WASHINGTON, D.C.

"ABANDON ALL HOPE
YE WHO ENTER HERE."
~ DANTE

WASHINGTON, D.C.

Too small to be a state but too large to be an asylum for the mentally deranged.

> *Anne Gorsuch Burford (1942–2004), mother of Supreme Court justice Neil Gorsuch and first woman administrator of the Environmental Protection Agency (remarks to a wool growers convention in Vail, Colorado, July 27, 1984)*

Sad to say some of our folks went to Washington to drain the swamp and made partnership with the alligators instead.

> *Fred Thompson (1942–2015), senator from Tennessee, actor (quoting a friend in Washington, in a speech at a political fund raiser in Columbia, South Carolina, June 27, 2007)*

The people who hate Trump the most are the people who have been running Washington for decades.

> *Glenn Greenwald (1967–), lawyer, journalist, blogger (quoted in Ian Parker, "The Bane of Their Resistance," New Yorker, September 3, 2018)*

WOMEN'S ISSUES

Because I am a woman, I must make unusual efforts to succeed. If I fail, no one will say, "She doesn't have what it takes"; they will say, "Women don't have what it takes."

> *Clare Boothe Luce (1903–1987), playwright, Republican congresswoman from Connecticut, ambassador to Italy* (Time *magazine obituary, December 28, 1987)*

It should be, but somehow isn't, an embarrassment to the feminist sisterhood chanting for Hillary, Hillary, Hillary, that right from the beginning hers was a "coattail career."

> *Roger Kimball (1953–), editor, author, and publisher,* The New Criterion *("Explaining Hillary Clinton's Appeal," PJ Media, April 2, 2015. The coattails in question belonged to Bill Clinton.)*

Donald Trump's support from white women is part of a huge realignment.

> *Jill Lepore (1966–), history professor, Harvard University (quoted in Scott Porch, "Jill Lepore: Politicians Can Dupe Voters but not Posterity," Daily Beast, October 19, 2018)*

Index of Subjects

ABOUT THE AUTHOR

Garry Apgar served as a Marine officer in Vietnam from April 1968 to July 1970. A former cartoonist and staff artist with the *Roanoke Times*, he has contributed drawings and articles to *National Review, The Weekly Standard, New York Times, Art in America* and *Le Monde*, among other publications. He earned a B.A. in French at Washington & Lee University, a Master's in Lettres Modernes from the Sorbonne, and a Ph.D. in the history of art from Yale. He has taught art history at Brown University, Princeton, the University of Delaware and the Université de Lyon.

His most recent books, *A Mickey Mouse Reader* (University Press of Mississippi, 2014) and *Mickey Mouse: Emblem of the American Spirit* (Walt Disney Family Foundation Press, 2015), were favorably reviewed in *The Weekly Standard, Wired, The Times Literary Supplement* and *City Journal*. Garry is currently President of The Voltaire Society of America. He has co-edited *The Quotable Voltaire*, which Bucknell University Press will publish later this year or early next year.

He lives in the Black Rock section of Bridgeport, Connecticut.